Jennifer Preschern

Skill Areas: Articulation, Language, and Literacy
Age Level: 4 through 9
Grades: Pre-K through 4th

LinguiSystems, Inc.
3100 4th Avenue
East Moline, IL 61244

800-776-4332

FAX: 800-577-4555
E-mail: service@linguisystems.com
Web: linguisystems.com

Copyright © 2004 LinguiSystems, Inc.

All of our products are copyrighted to protect the fine work of our authors. You may only copy the student pages as needed for your own use with students. Any other reproduction or distribution of the pages in this book is prohibited, including copying the entire book to use as another primary source or "master" copy.

Printed in the U.S.A.

ISBN 10: 0-7606-0517-3
ISBN 13: 978-0-7606-0517-2

About the Author

Jennifer Preschern, M.A., CCC-SLP, is a speech-language pathologist working for an elementary school on the north shore of Chicago. She has master's degrees from Northwestern University in speech-language pathology and in learning disabilities. Jennifer enjoys exploring the connection between spoken and written language and helping children become aware of their potential.

Dedication

To my parents, Clare and Max, and my brother, Tim, for their tireless love, encouragement, and positive attitudes. Also dedicated to my husband, Richard, who makes me want to be a better woman.

Cover Design by Mike Paustian
Edited by Barb Truman
Page Layout by Jamie Bellagamba
Illustrations by Margaret Warner

Table of Contents

Introduction	5
Family Letters	9
Articulation Hierarchy and Home Practice Ideas	14

/s/ Stories and Activities

Singing Sam	15
Articulation Cards	24
Sight Words Worksheet	25
Picture Searches	26
Writing Activity	29
Barrier Game	30
The Missing School Supplies	32
Articulation Cards	43
Sight Words Worksheet	44
Picture Searches	45
Writing Activity	48
Barrier Game	49
Going to the Beach	51
Articulation Cards	61
Sight Words Worksheet	62
Picture Searches	63
Writing Activity	66
Barrier Game	67

/r/ Stories and Activities

Running Rick	69
Articulation Cards	79
Sight Words Worksheet	80
Picture Searches	81
Writing Activity	84
Barrier Game	85
Reading Is Fun!	87
Articulation Cards	96
Sight Words Worksheet	97
Picture Searches	98
Writing Activity	101
Barrier Game	102
The Many Colors of Shoes	104
Articulation Cards	112
Sight Words Worksheet	113
Picture Searches	114
Writing Activity	117
Barrier Game	118

Table of Contents, continued

/l/ Stories and Activities

Lisa Likes to Play 120
    Articulation Cards 129
    Sight Words Worksheet 130
    Picture Searches 131
    Writing Activity 134
    Barrier Game 135

Mrs. Little 137
    Articulation Cards 146
    Sight Words Worksheet 147
    Picture Searches 148
    Writing Activity 151
    Barrier Game 152

Where Do You Live? 154
    Articulation Cards 164
    Sight Words Worksheet 165
    Picture Searches 166
    Writing Activity 169
    Barrier Game 170

Sample Tracking Form—Productions 172
Tracking Form—Productions 173
Sample Tracking Form—Percentages 174
Tracking Form—Percentages 175

Introduction

It is well known that children with early speech-language impairments may also have difficulty learning to read. As speech-language pathologists (SLPs) accept more responsibility for literacy development, the question arises, "How can I work on reading and writing without discontinuing other speech-language goals?" *Just for Kids: Articulation Stories* was created to help.

Contents

Just for Kids: Articulation Stories consists of nine thematic units containing stories and activities suitable for beginning readers. The lessons that follow each story can be reproduced and used as part of therapy or as homework. Family letters, pages 9-13, will help parents and caregivers understand and complete home practice. Each unit contains:

- a story loaded with the target phoneme in all positions
- a set of 10 reproducible picture cards for drill or games
- a worksheet to reinforce the sight words in the story
- picture search worksheets that focus on the target phoneme in each word position (initial, medial, final)
- a worksheet to extend the story into a written activity
- a barrier game for carryover

Articulation Therapy

The stories and activities were designed to provide practice for three of the most commonly misarticulated sounds: /s/, /r/, and /l/ in all word positions (initial, medial, final). You can focus work on one position per session by finding these target words in the stories or by using the picture search activities included in each unit. Suggested target words are listed at the bottom of the story and picture search pages. (You might challenge your students to find additional words for extra practice.) The tracking forms on pages 173 and 175 can be used to measure growth in each position. Examples of how to fill out these forms are on pages 172 and 174.

Literacy Work

The stories included in *Just for Kids: Articulation Stories* can help you provide intervention for the /s/, /r/, and /l/ sounds while simultaneously developing early reading skills, including sounding out phonetically regular words, memorizing common non-phonetic words, and using context to predict text. During speech-language therapy sessions, these stories can be treated as part of a guided reading lesson. First, you can do a "picture walk" through the story. Take time to describe the pictures in the story, predict the words in the text, and identify uncommon words. Then read the text with the student while encouraging the student to use strategies for any difficult word: sound it out, look for a phonetic pattern, and use the pictures. After each attempt, ask the student if the new guess makes sense.

Introduction, *continued*

These stories were developed with the early reader in mind. The majority of the words in the texts are high-frequency words from children's books. These words can be called "sight words" as children should recognize them instantly. Some of these sight words are phonetically regular (i.e., easy to sound out) and some are not. The rest of the words in the texts contain the target phonemes and can be predicted from the pictures.

Each unit also contains a writing activity that requires the student to use the target sound. Young students can orally dictate a story to practice carryover, write one or two sentences to answer the prompt, and/or draw a picture and describe it, using the target sound. Older students can write short essays and then read the essays to work on carryover.

Other Speech-Language Goals

In addition to meeting literacy and articulation goals, these stories can complement a speech-language caseload in other ways. The stories can be used as part of a phonemic awareness program. For instance, you can use the stories and activities to teach initial sound awareness. Since each story is loaded with a target phoneme, you can read a story to an entire class and have the students search for the target phoneme in the words and pictures. Then you or the classroom teacher can have each child design a picture using the barrier activity materials. Each child can cut, paste, and color the picture and take it home to share with family.

The stories can also be used to work on grammar and basic concepts. For example, in "The Many Colors of Shoes," personal pronouns are stressed (e.g., *he, she, it, her, ours*) and "Lisa Likes to Play" contains a number of prepositions (e.g., *in, with, under*). By reading the stories and completing the worksheets, these language skills will be reinforced.

The barrier activity materials can also be used to teach a number of receptive and expressive language goals. For example, you can use the barrier materials from "Singing Sam" to teach following directions and/or sequencing skills. You can take turns with the student to give directions on how to dress Sam using the materials and in what order.

With a little creativity, these materials can be used in many ways. Some suggested lesson plans are included on pages 7 and 8.

Introduction, continued

Lesson Plans

The following are suggested lesson plans for four 30-minute sessions using materials provided in this book. You will need to make copies of the cards and barrier game sheets in each unit.

Lesson 1:

(5 minutes) Introduce the story. Look for pictures with the target sound. Describe what is happening in each picture. Predict what might happen next. Look for uncommon or difficult words and identify their meanings.

(10 minutes) Read the story with the child. Encourage the child to use reading strategies to identify new words.

(5 minutes) Drill the target phoneme with the articulation cards provided following the story.

(5 minutes) Begin a homework sheet. Send the sheet home for continued practice.

Lesson 2:

(5 minutes) Check the speech homework and review what the child remembers from the story.

(5 minutes) Review any words the child struggled to decode during the previous lesson.

(10 minutes) Drill the target words from the story.

(5 minutes) Re-read the story together (or let the child read it aloud).

(5 minutes) Begin a homework activity sheet and send it home for continued practice.

Lesson 3:

(5 minutes) Check the speech homework.

(5 minutes) Re-read the story with the child (or let the child read it aloud).

(15 minutes) Using two copies of the articulation cards, play a game such as "Memory" or "Go Fish."

(5 minutes) Begin a homework activity sheet for the child to complete at home and/or send home a copy of the story for the child to read at home.

Introduction, *continued*

Lesson 4:

(5 minutes)   Check and review the speech homework.

(5 minutes)   Let the child read the story aloud to you.

(20 minutes) Using two copies of the barrier activity, name all the pictures. Point out the target sound in the pictures. Next place a visual barrier between you and the student. As the student completes his picture, have him describe what he is doing (e.g., "Place the shirt with the seven on Sam. Then put on the pants."). Remind the student to focus on correct production of target sounds. Then take down the barrier and compare your pictures. If you follow his description, and his description is accurate, your pictures will be identical.

I hope the addition of *Just for Kids: Articulation Stories* to your professional library provides you with a valuable and fun resource that will allow you to effectively address your clients' expanding needs.

                                                               Jennifer

Family Letter #1

Dear _____,

As part of my articulation therapy program, I will be sending home activities for you to work on with your child. Articulation therapy begins with saying target sounds in isolation (no words). As your child improves, we will work on sounds within words, then in sentences, and finally in conversation.

The level I will ask you to practice at home will always be one step easier than what we are working on in therapy. During home practice, please only practice at the level I have indicated. For instance, if the "word level" is indicated, do not try to correct the target sound(s) in your child's conversation. This will inevitably lead to frustration for both you and/or your child. I've attached a sheet with some tips for each level. Please call me with any questions.

Sincerely,

_____ _____
Speech-Language Pathologist   Date

Note: The tip sheet for parents (*Articulation Hierarchy and Home Practice Ideas*) can be found on page 14.

Family Letter #2

Dear _____,

In speech class, your child is practicing the sound _____. For home practice, please use the attached cards to play "Go Fish" with your child. Here is a suggestion of how to play:

1. Go through the deck and name each picture.

2. Shuffle the deck.

3. Give each player four cards. Put the rest of the cards facedown in a pile.

4. Take turns asking the other player for a card that matches one of yours. If the other player has the card, he/she gives it to you. Place the match beside you on the table. If not, take a card from the facedown pile. Then it's the other person's turn. At the end of the game (when someone runs out of cards), the person with the most matches wins.

While you play, please have your child practice the _____ sound as follows:

❑ Say the word on each card when a match is made.

❑ Make a sentence about each picture when a match is made.

❑ _____.

Thanks!

_____   _____
Speech-Language Pathologist   Date

Family Letter #3

Dear _____,

In speech class, your child and I have been reading the attached story. For home practice, please let your child read this story with you. When your child is finished, have him/her do the following:

- ❑ Find the _____ words and pictures and say them.

- ❑ Find the _____ words and pictures and make up one sentence about each one.

- ❑ Talk about the story with you. Please listen for the _____ sound in your child's speech. Talk about how your child did and practice any missed words.

Thanks!

_____   _____
Speech-Language Pathologist   Date

Family Letter #4

Dear _____,

In speech class, your child and I have been reading the story _____ _____. For homework, have your child complete the attached writing assignment about this story. After your child is finished, he/she can practice articulation as follows:

- ❏ Find the _____ words in the story and in the pictures. Practice saying these words.

- ❏ Find the _____ words in the story and in the pictures. Make up sentences using each of these words or read the sentences that contain these words. After each sentence, comment on how your child did and practice any missed words.

- ❏ Talk about the story or read the entire story. Please listen for the _____ sound in your child's speech. Comment on how your child does and practice any missed words.

Thanks!

_____   _____
Speech-Language Pathologist   Date

Family Letter #5

Dear _____,

In speech class, your child and I have been working on the sound _____ at the conversation level. Attached is a fun activity for you to do at home that will target the _____ sound in your child's conversation.

The goal of the activity is for you and your child to create two identical pictures by only using words and not by looking. Before you practice, place a visual barrier, such as an upright folder or book, between you and your child. Take turns describing and listening. The describer makes his/her picture and then describes it to the listener to recreate while saying the _____ sound correctly. Then take down the barrier and compare your pictures.

While you are playing, listen for your child's _____ sound. After each turn, practice any words that he/she missed.

Thanks!

_____   _____
Speech-Language Pathologist   Date

Articulation Hierarchy and Home Practice Ideas

1. Sound in Isolation Level

In speech class, we will practice producing the target sound by itself (e.g., *sssss*).

At home you can heighten your child's awareness of the target sound during a structured period every day. Read the speech story or another favorite story to your child and lengthen/accentuate every target sound. Have your child identify words in your speech that have the target sound. Do not expect your child to practice throughout the day as this would be frustrating for both of you. Instead, create a special "speech time" during the day when you and your child can practice.

2. Word Level

In therapy, I will ask your child to produce target words with varying levels of help. At first I will have your child say the words after me and show him/her how to make the sound. As time progresses, I will provide models less frequently. Eventually, I will expect your child to say words that contain his/her sound independently. Some ideas for home practice follow:

- ❑ Practice saying the speech words for 5 minutes every day.
- ❑ Draw pictures of the target words and/or find pictures in magazines and newspapers.
- ❑ Read books with your child and have him/her find words with the target sound. After you find the words, have your child pronounce these words.

3. Sentence Level

In speech, I will ask your child to say and then make up sentences with words that contain his/her target sound while providing varying levels of help, much like the word level. At first, I may ask your child to repeat short phrases in which only one word changes. As your child improves, I will ask him/her to say longer sentences. Eventually, I will have your child create his/her own sentences. Some ideas for home practice follow:

- ❑ Make up silly sentences or rhymes with the target words.
- ❑ Read books with your child and ask your child questions that require a response using a word with the target sound.
- ❑ Listen to familiar songs with your child. Find words in the songs with the target sound. Have your child practice saying lines from the song with the target sound.

4. Conversation Level

In speech, I will be structuring activities in a way that allows your child to say the target sound many times during a structured conversation.

At home, do not expect 100% accuracy all the time. Also, please do not make your child repeat a word until the sound is perfect. This can be very frustrating for you and your child. Instead, brainstorm a list of words with your child that contain the target sound. Then tell your child, "Let's talk about your day. Let's see how many of these words you can use."

Singing Sam

1

/s/ words: Sam, sing, sun, glasses, notes, socks, shorts, stripes, scooter, slide, swing, snake

Sam likes to sing.

2

/s/ words: Sam, sing, soap, sun, sink, glasses, faucet, notes, socks, shorts, stripes, snake, stars

Sam sings to his mom.

3

/s/ words: Sam, sing, salt, soup, sandwich, glasses, notes, socks, shorts, dress, lettuce, stripes, scarf, stove, spoons, spider, snake

Sam sings to his dad.

4

/s/ words: Sam, sing, sandwich, sun, sidewalk, sunglasses, mustache, bathing suit, glasses, muscles, outside, notes, shorts, socks, grass, house, stripes

Sam sings to his sister.

5

/s/ words: Sam, sing, soccer ball, seven, soup, sidewalk, glasses, braces, sister, notes, grass, cleats, socks, shorts, stripes, stop sign, scooter, scarf, smile, store

Sam sings to his cat.

6

/s/ words: Sam, sing, sailboat, sandwich, glasses, socks, shorts, notes, fireplace, vase, tulips, mouse, lettuce, sleep, snake, stripes

Sam sings to his dog.

7

/s/ words: Sam, sing, glasses, biscuit, outside, notes, grass, fence, doghouse, shorts, socks, spots, slide, swings, stripes

Sam sings to his fish.

8

/s/ words: Sam, sing, sofa, scissors, kissing, glasses, baseball, basketball, notes, socks, shorts, stripes, skis

Sam sings himself to sleep.

9

/s/ words: Sam, sing, dinosaurs, glasses, poster, books, notes, stuffed dinosaur, desk, asleep/sleep

/s/ Articulation Cards

Cut apart these cards and use them for drill or games.

sing

soup

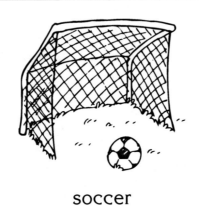
soccer

soap

glasses

baseball

basketball

grass

mouse

fireplace

/s/ Sight Words   Name _____

Complete these sentences. Use the words in the Word Bank to fill in the blanks.

1. This is Sam.

2. This is _____ dog.

Word Bank

his

to

3. Sam sings _____ his dog.

4. This is _____ mom.

5. Sam sings _____ his mom.

6. This is _____ dad.

7. Sam sings _____ his dad.

Family: After your child completes this worksheet, practice saying /s/ in:

☐ words—Practice these words: Sam, sing, _____.

☐ sentences—Read the sentences above.

☐ conversation—Talk about things Sam does in the story.

Singing Sam—/s/
Just For Kids: Articulation Stories

/s/ Picture Search

Name _____

Find at least five things that have an /s/ sound in the beginning of the word. Circle them.

Family: Please practice the /s/ sound in:

❏ words—Name each /s/ picture _____ times.

❏ sentences—Make up _____ sentences about each /s/ picture.

❏ conversation—Talk about the picture. What is Sam's sister using as her goal?

Answer: salt, soup, sink, Sam, sandwich, seven, sister, scarf, spots, snake, soccer, spoon

Singing Sam—/s/
Just For Kids: Articulation Stories

/s/ Picture Search

Name _____

Find at least five things that have an /s/ sound in the middle of the word. Circle them.

Family: Please practice the /s/ sound in:

❑ words—Say each /s/ picture _____ times.

❑ sentences—Make up _____ sentences about each /s/ picture.

❑ conversation—Talk about the picture. Where do you think Sam's dad is going?

Answer: kissing, glasses, baseball, muscles, desk, basketball

Singing Sam—/s/
Just For Kids: Articulation Stories 27 Copyright © 2004 LinguiSystems, Inc.

/s/ Picture Search

Name _____

Find at least five things that have an /s/ sound at the end of the word. Circle them.

Family: Please practice the /s/ sound in:

☐ words—Say each /s/ picture _____ times.

☐ sentences—Make up _____ sentences about each /s/ picture.

☐ conversation—Talk about the picture. What do you think is happening?

Answer: shorts, dress, doghouse, mouse, tulips, grass, house, fence, spots

Singing Sam—/s/
Just For Kids: Articulation Stories

/s/ Writing Activity   Name _____

In the story, "Singing Sam," Sam likes to sing all day long. What do you like to do all day long?

Think of things you do that have an /s/ sound. Here are some ideas to get you started: study, sports, dance.

☐   Draw a picture of something you like to do.

☐   Write about it.

_____
_____
_____
_____
_____
_____

Singing Sam—/s/
Just For Kids: Articulation Stories

/s/ Barrier Game

Name _____

Use this page with the pictures on page 31.

Singing Sam—/s/
Just For Kids: Articulation Stories

/s/ Barrier Game, continued   Name _____

Cut out these pictures and use them to dress Sam on page 30.

The Missing School Supplies

1

/s/ words: sign, scissors, pencil, eraser, missing, grass, kites, spider, school, stapler, slide, swings, sky, spots, school supplies, string

Spotty, the spider, lost all of her school supplies.

2

/s/ words: sad, classroom, face, spots, Spotty, spider, school supplies, stand, desk, lost

Spotty asks Mouse, "May I use your scissors?"

3

/s/ words: sandals, scissors, bracelet, whiskers, Mouse, purse, necklace, dress, spots, Spotty, spider, straps, asks

Mouse says, "Yes."

4

/s/ words: says, scissors, bracelet, whiskers, necklace, purse, Mouse, yes, dress, spots, Spotty, strap

Spotty asks Squirrel, "May I use your pencil?"

/s/ words: scissors, pencil, shoelaces, whiskers, pants, spots, Spotty, spider, Squirrel, asks

Squirrel says, "Yes."

6

/s/ words: says, scissors, pencil, whiskers, yes, spots, Spotty, spider, Squirrel

Spotty asks Octopus, "May I use your eraser?"

7

/s/ words: scissors, pencil, eraser, Octopus, spots, Spotty, spider, scarf, stripes, basketball, desk, asks

Octopus says, "Yes."

8

/s/ words: says, scissors, pencil, eraser, yes, Octopus, spots, Spotty, spider, scarf, stripes, basketball

Spotty asks Seal, "May I use your stapler?"

9

/s/ words: scissors, Seal, suit, eraser, pencil, whiskers, thermos, cactus, spots, Spotty, spider, stapler, desk, asks

Seal says, "Yes."

/s/ words: Seal, suit, says, scissors, eraser, pencil, whiskers, yes, stapler, spots, Spotty, spider

Spotty does her work.

11

/s/ words: circles, scissors, pencil, eraser, spots, Spotty, spider, stapler, desk, squares

/s/ Articulation Cards

Cut apart these cards and use them for drill or games.

/s/ Sight Words   Name _____

Complete these sentences. Use the words in the Word Bank to fill in the blanks.

1. Spotty _____, "Hello!"

2. These are _____ scissors.

Word Bank

may

your

says

3. _____ I use your scissors?

4. Where are _____ scissors?

5. Spotty _____, "Thanks!"

6. The teacher _____, "Do your work."

Family: After your child completes this worksheet, practice saying /s/ in:

❏ words—Practice these words: spider, scissors, _____.

❏ sentences—Read the sentences above.

❏ conversation—Talk about things Spotty does in the story.

/s/ Picture Search

Name _____

Find at least five things that have an /s/ sound in the beginning of the word. Circle them.

Family: Please practice the /s/ sound in:

❑ words—Say each /s/ picture _____ times.

❑ sentences—Make up _____ sentences about each /s/ picture.

❑ conversation—Talk about the picture. Where do you think Seal and Spotty are going?

Answer: sidewalk, sandals, suit, Seal, sunglasses, spider, spots, Spotty, stapler

The Missing School Supplies—/s/
Just For Kids: Articulation Stories

Copyright © 2004 LinguiSystems, Inc.

/s/ Picture Search

Name _____

Find at least five things that have an /s/ sound in the middle of the word. Circle them.

Family: Please practice the /s/ sound in:

❏ words—Say each /s/ picture _____ times.

❏ sentences—Make up _____ sentences about each /s/ picture.

❏ conversation—Talk about the picture. How do you think Spotty lost her school supplies?

Answer: baseball, pencil, eraser, bracelet, basketball, whiskers

The Missing School Supplies—/s/
Just For Kids: Articulation Stories

/s/ Picture Search

Name _____

Find at least five things that have an /s/ sound at the end of the word. Circle them.

Family: Please practice the /s/ sound in:

☐ words—Say each /s/ picture _____ times.

☐ sentences—Make up _____ sentences about each /s/ picture.

☐ conversation—Talk about the picture.

Answer: Mouse, purse, thermos, necklace, happy face, dress, spots, straps

/s/ Writing Activity

Name _____

In the story, "The Missing School Supplies," Spotty asks her friends if she can use their school supplies. Her friends are all animals with an /s/ sound in their names.

Think of people you know who have an /s/ sound in their names.

☐ Draw a picture of one of these people.

☐ Write about this person.

_____
_____
_____
_____
_____
_____

/s/ Barrier Game

Name _____

Use this page with the pictures on page 50.

/s/ Barrier Game, continued   Name _____

Cut out the animals and put them on the playground on page 49.

The Missing School Supplies—/s/
Just For Kids: Articulation Stories

/s/ words: sand, sun, sand castle, starfish, sky

Max and Sarah go to the beach.

2

/s/ words: Sarah, sign, side, city, sandals, sunglasses, bicycle, dice, Max, shorts, bus, dress, steps, straps, stripes, skyline

Max sees a sailboat.

3

/s/ words: sailboat, sail, seal, sees, sunglasses, dinosaur, Max, scarf, stripes

Sarah sees a surfer.

4

/s/ words: Sarah, sees, surfer, surfboard, sandals, sunglasses, dress, snake, snail, stripes, straps

Max sees a snail.

5

/s/ words: sun, sees, sand, sunglasses, Max, snail

Sarah sees a restaurant.

6

/s/ words: Sarah, sees, sign, sandals, sidewalk, restaurant, cactus, dress, stripes, straps

Sarah and Max eat soup.

7

/s/ words: Sarah, soup, salt, sunglasses, restaurant, cactus, Max, spoon, stripes

They eat salad.

8

/s/ words: Sarah, salad, dressing, sunglasses, Max, lettuce, cactus, stripes

They eat sandwiches.

9

/s/ words: Sarah, Sally, sandwich, sunglasses, ice, Max, waitress, straw, stripes

Sarah and Max sit in the sun.

10

/s/ words: Sarah, sit, sun, setting, sand, seagulls, sand castle, sunglasses, dinosaur, six, Max, swimsuits, sunscreen, starfish, stripes, straw

/s/ Articulation Cards

Cut apart these cards and use them for drill or games.

sailboat

 surfer	 sandal	 bathing suit
 sand castle	 bicycle	 dress
 cactus	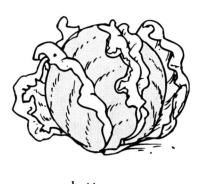 ice	lettuce

/s/ Sight Words   Name _____

Complete these sentences. Use the words in the Word Bank to fill in the blanks.

1. Max and Sarah go to _____ beach.

2. _____ see a sailboat.

Word Bank

they

see

the

3. They _____ a surfer.

4. _____ eat soup.

5. They sit in _____ sun.

6. They _____ a snail.

Family: After your child completes this worksheet, practice saying /s/ in:

☐ words—Practice these words: see, soup, sun, _____.

☐ sentences—Read the sentences above.

☐ conversation—Discuss the things you can see at the beach.

/s/ Picture Search

Name _____

Find at least five things that have an /s/ sound in the beginning of the word. Circle them.

Family: Please practice the /s/ sound in:

❑ words—Say each /s/ picture _____ times.

❑ sentences—Make up _____ sentences about each /s/ picture.

❑ conversation—Talk about the picture.

Answer: sailboat, surfer, sun, seagull, seal, Sarah, surfboard, sunglasses, scarf, snake, sky, stripes

/s/ Picture Search

Name _____

Find at least five things that have an /s/ sound in the middle of the word. Circle them.

Family: Please practice the /s/ sound in:

☐ words—Say each /s/ picture _____ times.

☐ sentences—Make up _____ sentences about each /s/ picture.

☐ conversation—Talk about the picture. What are Max and Sarah making?

Answer: whistle, bathing suit, dinosaur, bicycle, sand castle

Going to the Beach—/s/
Just For Kids: Articulation Stories

/s/ Picture Search

Name _____

Find at least five things that have an /s/ sound at the end of the word.
Circle them.

Family: Please practice the /s/ sound in:

❏ words—Say each /s/ picture _____ times.

❏ sentences—Make up _____ sentences about each /s/ picture.

❏ conversation—Talk about the picture. What is the waitress going to do with the lettuce?

Answer: cactus, ice, lettuce, waitress, horse, glass, fence

Going to the Beach—/s/
Just For Kids: Articulation Stories

/s/ Writing Activity

Name _____

In the story, "Going to the Beach," Sarah and Max see many things that have an /s/ sound.

Think of things you see at _____ that have an /s/ sound.

☐ Draw a picture of them.

☐ Write about one of them.

/s/ Barrier Game

Name _____

Use this page with the pictures on page 68.

Going to the Beach—/s/
Just For Kids: Articulation Stories

/s/ Barrier Game, continued   Name _____

Cut out these pictures and put them on the scene on page 67.

Going to the Beach—/s/
Just For Kids: Articulation Stories

/r/ words: run, Rick, roses, rake, shirt, shorts, star, tree

Rick runs very fast.

2

/r/ words: Rick, run, very, shirt, shorts, car, pear, star

Rick runs to the door.

3

/r/ words: Rick, run, classroom, first, shirt, shorts, star, door, pear, teacher, grade, angry

Rick runs into the classroom.

4

/r/ words: Rick, run, room, row, write, classroom, first, shirt, shorts, star, pear, teacher, angry, grade

Rick runs to his locker.

5

/r/ words: Rick, run, locker, shirt, shorts, star, pear, four, three, trip

Rick runs to art class.

6

/r/ words: Rick, run, art, parrot, butterfly, shirt, shorts, star, pear, paper, picture, drop, paintbrushes

Rick runs to recess.

7

/r/ words: Rick, run, recess, jump rope, four square, monkey bars, shirt, shorts, playground

Rick runs to the water fountain.

8

/r/ words: Rick, run, girl, shirt, shorts, water fountain

Rick runs to the library.

9

/r/ words: Rick, run, Ron, doorway, principal, library, library card

Rick needs to rest.
10

/r/ words: Rick, rest, snoring, shirt, shorts, jump rope, pear, chair

/r/ Articulation Cards

Cut apart these cards and use them for drill or games.

/r/ Sight Words

Name _____

Complete these sentences. Use the words in the Word Bank to fill in the blanks.

1. Rick likes to _____.

2. Rick runs very _____.

Word Bank

run

runs

very

fast

3. Rick _____ to his classroom.

4. Rick likes to _____ to his locker.

5. Rick _____ to art class.

6. Rick is _____ tired.

Family: After your child completes this worksheet, practice saying /r/ in:

☐ words—Practice these words: Rick, run, classroom, locker, art, tired, _____.

☐ sentences—Read the sentences above.

☐ conversation—Talk about where Rick runs. What would happen if you ran to these places?

/r/ Picture Search

Name _____

Find at least five things that have an /r/ sound in the beginning of the word. Circle them.

Family: Please practice the /r/ sound in:

☐ words—Say each /r/ picture _____ times.

☐ sentences—Make up _____ sentences about each /r/ picture.

☐ conversation—Talk about the picture. Where do you think Rick is going?

Answer: Rick, rake, rose, rabbit, radio, radish, rainbow

Running Rick—/r/
Just For Kids: Articulation Stories

/r/ Picture Search   Name _____

Find at least five things that have an /r/ sound in the middle of the word. Circle them.

Family: Please practice the /r/ sound in:

- ❑ words—Say each /r/ picture _____ times.

- ❑ sentences—Make up _____ sentences about each /r/ picture.

- ❑ conversation—What is happening in the picture?

Answer: jump rope, parrot, art, purse, butterfly, girl

/r/ Picture Search

Name _____

Find at least five things that have an /r/ sound at the end of the word. Circle them.

Family: Please practice the /r/ sound in:

☐ words—Say each /r/ picture _____ times.

☐ sentences—Make up _____ sentences about each /r/ picture.

☐ conversation—What is happening in the picture?

Answer: four, pear, locker, teacher, door

/r/ Writing Activity   Name _____

In the story, "Running Rick," Rick likes to run.

Think of something you like to do that has an /r/ sound. Here are some ideas to get you started: read, write, soccer, draw.

☐ Draw a picture of it.

☐ Write about it.

_____

_____

_____

_____

_____

_____

/r/ Barrier Game   Name _____

Use this page with the pictures on page 86.

/r/ Barrier Game, continued   Name _____

Cut out these rooms and put them on page 85 to make Rick's school.

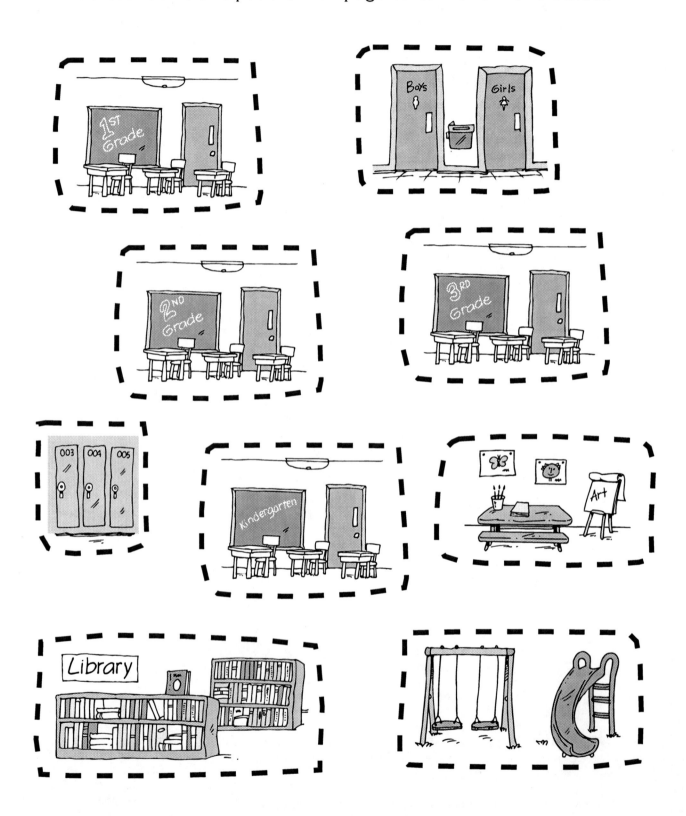

Running Rick—/r/
Just For Kids: Articulation Stories

Reading Is Fun!

1

/r/ words: read, ribbon, girl, carrot, hair, monster, cover

She likes to read.

2

/r/ words: read, rabbit, ribbon, girl, wearing, hair, cover

He likes to read.

3

/r/ words: read, skateboarding, cover, car, pear

She likes to read.

4

/r/ words: read, rose, girl, bird, flower, hair, cover, hamburger, tree, three

They like to read.

5

/r/ words: read, rocket, girl, butterfly, airplane, cover, flower, four, teddy bear, braces

They like to read too.

6

/r/ words: read, rice, girl, pyramid, carrot, yogurt, four, pear, candy bar, hamburger, bread

It likes to eat books.

/r/ words: rip, hairy, monster, cover, more

Run!

/r/ words: run, rabbit, scared, hairy, monster, cover

/r/ words: reading, rabbit, hairy, monster

/r/ Articulation Cards

Cut apart these cards and use them for drill or games.

read

rocket

rabbit

three

bird

carrot

four

monster

hamburger

pear

/r/ Sight Words   Name _____

Complete these sentences. Use the words in the Word Bank to fill in the blanks.

1. _____ read one book.

2. _____ reads two books.

Word Bank

3. _____ reads three books.

| he |
| she |
| it |
| they |
| we |
| I |

4. _____ read four books.

5. _____ read five books.

6. _____ eats the books.

7. _____ all run!

Family: After your child completes this worksheet, practice saying /r/ in:
- ☐ words—Practice these words: read, three, four, _____.
- ☐ sentences—Read the sentences above.
- ☐ conversation—How many books can you read? Name some books with the /r/ sound in the titles.

/r/ Picture Search

Name _____

Find at least five things that have an /r/ sound in the beginning of the word. Circle them.

Family: Please practice the /r/ sound in:

☐ words—Say each /r/ picture _____ times.

☐ sentences—Make up _____ sentences about each /r/ picture.

☐ conversation—Talk about the picture.

Answer: ribbon, rocket, rice, rabbit, rose, Little Red Riding Hood

Reading Is Fun!—/r/
Just For Kids: Articulation Stories

/r/ Picture Search

Name _____

Find at least five things that have an /r/ sound in the middle of the word. Circle them.

Family: Please practice the /r/ sound in:

☐ words—Say each /r/ picture _____ times.

☐ sentences—Make up _____ sentences about each /r/ picture.

☐ conversation—Talk about the picture. What are some healthy foods you like that have an /r/ sound?

Answer: carrot, bird, airplane, butterfly, food pyramid, girl

Reading Is Fun!—/r/
Just For Kids: Articulation Stories
Copyright © 2004 LinguiSystems, Inc.

/r/ Picture Search

Name _____

Find at least five things that have an /r/ sound at the end of the word. Circle them.

Family: Please practice the /r/ sound in:

❏ words—Say each /r/ picture _____ times.

❏ sentences—Make up _____ sentences about each /r/ picture.

❏ conversation—Talk about the picture. What will the monster eat for lunch today?

Answer: car, monster, hamburger, four, bear, dollar, counter

Reading Is Fun!—/r/
Just For Kids: Articulation Stories

/r/ Writing Activity   Name _____

In the story, "Reading Is Fun!" the children read about things that have an /r/ sound. What books do you know that have an /r/ sound in the title? Here are some ideas to get you started: *Little Red Riding Hood*, *Goldilocks and the Three Bears*, *Cinderella*.

☐ Draw one of the book covers.

☐ Write about the book.

_____

_____

_____

_____

_____

_____

/r/ Barrier Game

Name _____

Use this page with the pictures on page 103. Give each book a title and tell what the book is about.

/r/ Barrier Game, continued   Name _____

Cut out these pictures and use them to decorate the books on page 102.

The Many Colors of Shoes

1

/r/ words: horseshoes, soccer shoe, color, pair, stripes

Note to teacher: Have your students color the shoes in this story to match the text. You might want to color the shoes ahead of time for your younger students.

The Many Colors of Shoes—/r/
Just For Kids: Articulation Stories

We wear shoes.
2

/r/ words: horse, wear, teacher, doctor, soccer player, flower, stripes

Our shoes are orange.
3

/r/ words: ribbon, circus, large, orange, our, are, flower, star, hair, tiger, stripes

Her shoes are red.

4

/r/ words: red, write, rectangle, circle, wearing, her, are, teacher, poster, sweater, chair, square, star, triangle

The Many Colors of Shoes—/r/
Just For Kids: Articulation Stories

His shoes are brown.

5

/r/ words: wearing, around, are, doctor, brown

Their shoes are green.

6

/r/ words: jersey, zero, soccer player/ball, their, are, number, four, three, green, stripes

Its shoes are gray.

7

/r/ words: rock, rose, horse, horseshoe, flower, are, gray

My shoes are _____.

8

/r/ words: large, shirt, shorts, are

/r/ Articulation Cards

Cut apart these cards and use them for drill or games.

		 rectangle
 red	 orange	 purple
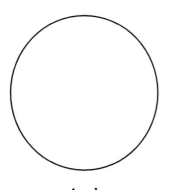 circle	 square	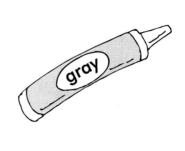 gray
 green	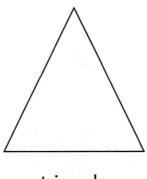 triangle	 brown

The Many Colors of Shoes—/r/
Just For Kids: Articulation Stories

/r/ Sight Words

Name _____

Complete these sentences. Use the words in the Word Bank to fill in the blanks. You will also need red, orange, green, brown, and gray crayons.

1. _____ shoes are orange.

Word Bank

its

our

their

his

her

2. _____ shoes are red.

3. _____ shoes are brown.

4. _____ shoes are green.

5. _____ shoes are gray.

6. My shoes are _____.

Family: After your child completes this worksheet, practice saying /r/ in:

❏ words—Practice these words: our, her, their, red, orange, _____.

❏ sentences—Read the sentences above.

❏ conversation—What color shoes do your family members wear? Describe the shoes.

The Many Colors of Shoes—/r/
Just For Kids: Articulation Stories

/r/ Picture Search   Name _____

Find at least five things that have an /r/ sound in the beginning of the word. Circle them.

Family: Please practice the /r/ sound in:

❐ words—Say each /r/ picture _____ times.

❐ sentences—Make up _____ sentences about each /r/ picture.

❐ conversation—Talk about the picture.

Answer: rock, ribbon, rose, ring, rake

/r/ Picture Search

Name _____

Find at least five things that have an /r/ sound in the middle of the word. Circle them.

Family: Please practice the /r/ sound in:

❏ words—Say each /r/ picture _____ times.

❏ sentences—Make up _____ sentences about each /r/ picture.

❏ conversation—What is happening in the picture?

Answer: circle, horse, carrot, butterfly, airplane, circus tent

The Many Colors of Shoes—/r/
Just For Kids: Articulation Stories

/r/ Picture Search

Name _____

Find at least five things that have an /r/ sound at the end of the word. Circle them.

Family: Please practice the /r/ sound in:

❏ words—Say each /r/ picture _____ times.

❏ sentences—Make up _____ sentences about each /r/ picture.

❏ conversation—Talk about the picture. What is the teacher doing?

Answer: star, flower, four, square, feather, poster

The Many Colors of Shoes—/r/
Just For Kids: Articulation Stories

/r/ Writing Activity

Name _____

In the story, "The Many Colors of Shoes," the colors all have an /r/ sound.

Think of other people and things you see in your school that have an /r/ sound. Here are some ideas to get you started: teacher, principal, ruler, calendar, rug.

☐ Draw one of things you see in your school that have an /r/ sound.

☐ Write about one of them.

_____

_____

_____

_____

_____

/r/ Barrier Game

Name _____

Use this page with the pictures on page 119.

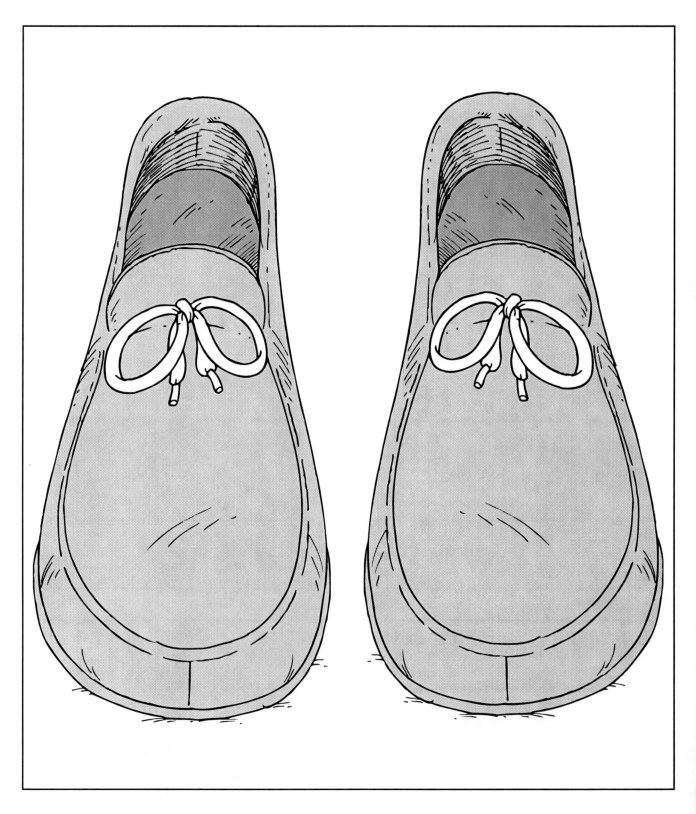

/r/ Barrier Game, continued   Name _____

Color and cut out these shapes. Use them to decorate the shoes on page 118.

Color these red.

  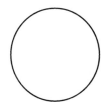  

Color these purple.

  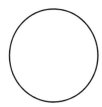 

Color these _____.

  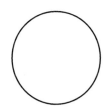  

Lisa Likes to Play

1

/l/ words: Lisa, like, lion, legs, smiling, apple, play, glasses

Lisa likes to play in the car.

2

/l/ words: Lisa, like, lion, lips, lipstick, cell phone, smiling, doll, play, Kleenex, glasses

Lisa likes to play on the slide.

3

/l/ words: Lisa, like, ladder, laughing, smiling, in-line skates, apple, slide, play, glasses

Lisa likes to play in the line.

4

/l/ words: Lisa, like, line, ball, apple, play, glasses, cloud

Lisa likes to play by her locker.

5

/l/ words: Lisa, like, locker, lion, eleven, smiling, balloon, ball, play, glasses

Lisa likes to play in her class.

6

/l/ words: Lisa, like, listen, calendar, smile, play, class, clapping, glasses

Lisa likes to play at the library.

7

/l/ words: Lisa, like, library, lion, librarian, telephone, tulips, Principal Lee, flag, play, globe

Lisa likes to play under the table.

8

/l/ words: Lisa, like, ladder, pencils, table, apple, play, blocks, glasses

Lisa likes to play all day!

9

/l/ words: Lisa, lion, pencils, in-line skates, balloon, all, doll, ball, apple, play, blocks, flag, glasses

/l/ Articulation Cards

Cut apart these cards and use them for drill or games.

line

library

locker

lips

in-line skates

calendar

table

doll

apple

pencil

/l/ Sight Words   Name _____

Complete these sentences. Use the words in the Word Bank to fill in the blanks.

1. Lisa is _____ the slide.

2. Lisa is _____ the line.

Word Bank

in

by

on

under

at

3. Lisa is _____ her desk.

4. Lisa is _____ the library.

5. Lisa is _____ her locker.

6. Lisa is _____ the table.

Family: After your child completes this worksheet, practice saying /l/ in:

❑ words—Practice these words: line, library, locker, table, _____.

❑ sentences—Read the sentences above.

❑ conversation—Talk about the places Lisa goes. Can you think of other places she can go that have an /l/ sound?

/l/ Picture Search

Name _____

Find at least five things that have an /l/ sound in the beginning of the word. Circle them.

Family: Please practice the /l/ sound in:

❏ words—Say each /l/ picture _____ times.

❏ sentences—Make up _____ sentences about each /l/ picture.

❏ conversation—What is happening in the picture?

Answer: lion, leg, ladder, library, Lisa, librarian

/l/ Picture Search   Name _____

Find at least five things that have an /l/ sound in the middle of the word. Circle them.

Family: Please practice the /l/ sound in:

❏ words—Say each /l/ picture _____ times.

❏ sentences—Make up _____ sentences about each /l/ picture.

❏ conversation—Talk about the picture.

Answer: in-line skates, elephant, balloon, calendar, hallway, cell phone (telephone)

Lisa Likes to Play—/l/
Just For Kids: Articulation Stories

/l/ Picture Search   Name _____

Find at least five things that have an /l/ sound at the end of the word. Circle them.

Family: Please practice the /l/ sound in:

☐ words—Say each /l/ picture _____ times.

☐ sentences—Make up _____ sentences about each /l/ picture.

☐ conversation—Talk about the picture. What do you think the principal and Lisa are talking about?

Answer: ball, table, principal, apple, snail

Lisa Likes to Play—/l/
Just For Kids: Articulation Stories

/l/ Writing Activity   Name _____

In the story, "Lisa Likes to Play," Lisa plays with things that have an /l/ sound.

Think of toys that have an /l/ sound. Here are some ideas to get you started: doll, in-line skates, blocks.

☐ Draw a picture of _____ of these toys.
                    number

☐ Write about one of these toys.

Lisa Likes to Play—/l/
Just For Kids: Articulation Stories

/l/ Barrier Game Name _____

Use this page with the pictures on page 136.

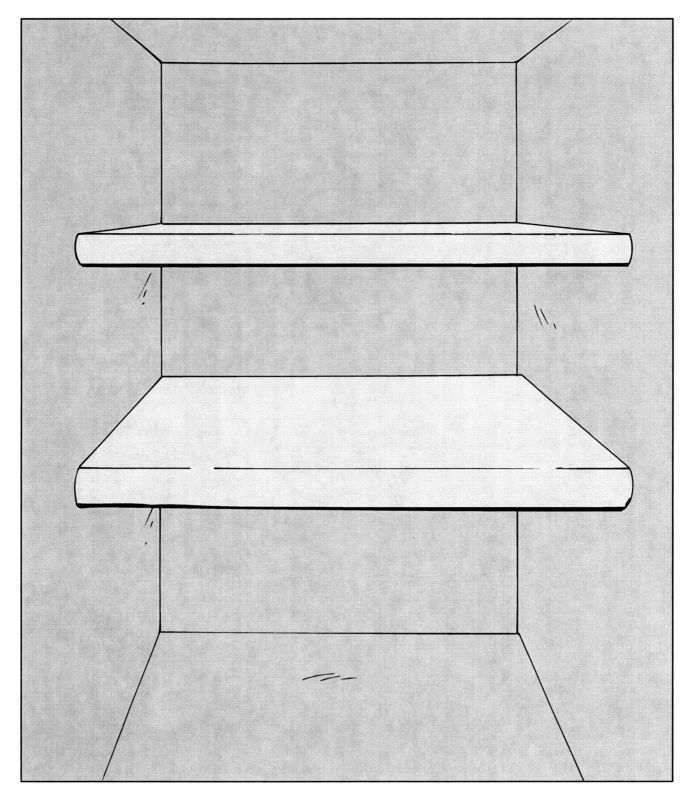

Lisa Likes to Play—/l/
Just For Kids: Articulation Stories

/l/ Barrier Game, continued   Name _____

Cut out these pictures. Help Lisa put them away in the closet on page 135.

Lisa Likes to Play—/l/
Just For Kids: Articulation Stories

Mrs. Little

1

/l/ words: lady, lips, long, Mrs. Little, eyelashes

Mrs. Little is a lady who lives by Luke.

2

/l/ words: lady, live, ladder, Luke, letter, Mrs. Little, tulips, mailbox, bracelet

Mrs. Little says, "Look up there."

3

/l/ words: Luke, lady, look, Mrs. Little, bracelet, balloons, clouds

Mrs. Little says, "Look down there."

4

/l/ words: lady, Luke, look, lifeguard, Mrs. Little, sunglasses, towel, pool, cloud

Mrs. Little says, "Look over there."

5

/l/ words: lady, Luke, look, lettuce, lemons, Mrs. Little, bracelet, apples, jelly

Mrs. Little says, "Look in there."

6

/l/ words: lady, Luke, look, sale, snail, crawling, Mrs. Little, glasses, clothes, gloves

Mrs. Little says, "Look out there."

7

/l/ words: lady, Luke, look, lamp, Mrs. Little, bracelet, jelly beans, table, clothes, clothespins

Luke looks out there.

8

/l/ words: Luke, look, lamp, table

Luke sees the world.

9

/l/ words: Luke, owl, world, tulips, balloons, apples, cloud

/l/ Articulation Cards

Cut apart these cards and use them for drill or games.

lifeguard

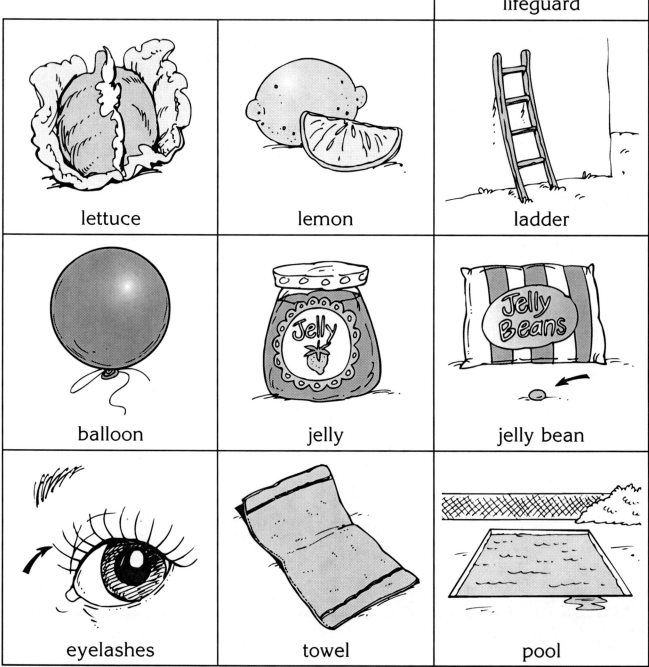

lettuce	lemon	ladder
balloon	jelly	jelly bean
eyelashes	towel	pool

/l/ Sight Words   Name _____

Complete these sentences. Use the words in the Word Bank to fill in the blanks.

1. The boy looks _____.

2. The balloon is _____ the sky.

Word Bank

up

down

over

in

out

3. The boy looks _____.

4. The girl is _____ the pool.

5. The boy looks _____ the window.

6. The gloves are _____ the window.

7. The balloon is _____ the apple tree.

Family: After your child completes this worksheet, practice saying /l/ in:

❏ words—Practice these words: look, balloon, girl, apple, _____.

❏ sentences—Read the sentences above.

❏ conversation—Talk about the things you see around the room. Are there things with an /l/ sound? Where are they?

/l/ Picture Search

Name _____

Find at least five things that have an /l/ sound in the beginning of the word. Circle them.

Family: Please practice the /l/ sound in:

❑ words—Say each /l/ picture _____ times.

❑ sentences—Make up _____ sentences about each /l/ picture.

❑ conversation—Talk about the picture.

Answer: lifeguard, lettuce, lemons, lobsters, lawnmower

Mrs. Little—/l/
Just For Kids: Articulation Stories

/l/ Picture Search

Name _____

Find at least five things that have an /l/ sound in the middle of the word. Circle them.

Family: Please practice the /l/ sound in:

❏ words—Say each /l/ picture _____ times.

❏ sentences—Make up _____ sentences about each /l/ picture.

❏ conversation—Talk about the picture.

Answer: bracelet, tulips, balloons, in-line skates, envelope, mailbox

/l/ Picture Search   Name _____

Find at least five things that have an /l/ sound at the end of the word. Circle them.

Family: Please practice the /l/ sound in:

☐ words—Say each /l/ picture _____ times.

☐ sentences—Make up _____ sentences about each /l/ picture.

☐ conversation—Talk about the picture.

Answer: pool, towel, apple, owl, ball, snail, girl

Mrs. Little—/l/
Just For Kids: Articulation Stories

/l/ Writing Activity   Name _____

In the story, "Mrs. Little," the lady shows the boy things with an /l/ sound.

Think of things you see at _____ that have an /l/ sound.

☐ Draw a picture of one of these things.

☐ Write about one of them.

_____
_____
_____
_____
_____
_____

/l/ Barrier Game

Name _____

Use this page with the pictures on page 153.

/l/ Barrier Game, continued   Name _____

Cut out these pictures and put them in Mrs. Little's yard on page 152.

Mrs. Little—/l/
Just For Kids: Articulation Stories

/l/ words: live, tulips, sidewalk, clouds

Where does the lion live?

2

/l/ words: lion, live, long, tail

The lion lives in the grassland.

3

/l/ words: lion, live, grassland, elephant, alligator

Where does the ladybug live?

4

/l/ words: ladybug, live, legs, smile

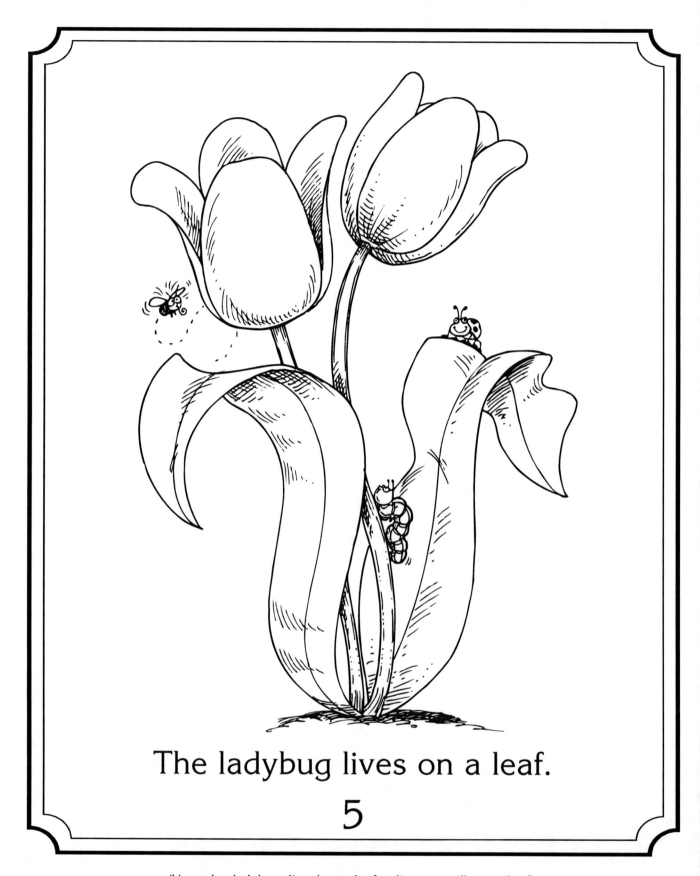

The ladybug lives on a leaf.
5

/l/ words: ladybug, live, large, leaf, tulip, caterpillar, smile, fly

Where does the owl live?

6

/l/ words: live, owl

The owl lives on a limb.

7

/l/ words: live, limb, owl, squirrel

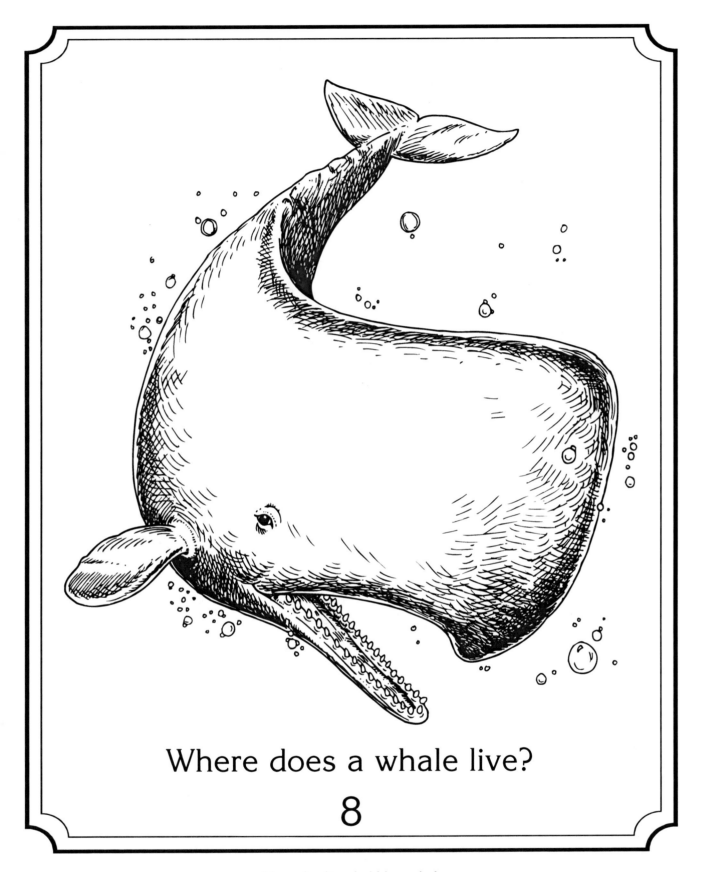

Where does a whale live?

8

/l/ words: live, bubbles, whale

A whale lives in the ocean.

9

/l/ words: live, lobster, bubbles, whale, clam

Where do you live?
10

/l/ words: live, smiling, sandals, girl

/l/ Articulation Cards

Cut apart these cards and use them for drill or games.

lion

ladybug

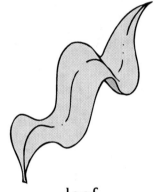
leaf

lobster

elephant

tulip

alligator

grassland

owl

whale

/l/ Sight Words   Name _____

Complete these sentences. Use the words in the Word Bank to fill in the blanks.

1. _____ does the lion live?

2. The lion lives _____ the grassland.

3. Where _____ the owl live?

Word Bank

where

live

does

in

lives

4. The owl _____ on a limb.

5. Where does the ladybug _____?

6. The ladybug _____ on a leaf.

7. Where _____ the whale live?

8. The whale lives _____ the water.

9. Where do you _____?

10. I live _____ _____.
    (Fill in your own word here.)

Family: After your child completes this worksheet, practice saying /l/ in:

☐ words—Practice these words: lion, live, leaf, owl, _____.

☐ sentences—Read the sentences above.

☐ conversation—Talk about the places where these animals live. What kinds of things can you see in these places? Can you think of things that have an /l/ sound?

/l/ Picture Search

Name _____

Find at least five things that have an /l/ sound in the beginning of the word. Circle them.

Family: Please practice the /l/ sound in:

❑ words—Say each /l/ picture _____ times.

❑ sentences—Make up _____ sentences about each /l/ picture.

❑ conversation—Talk about the picture. What are the animals doing?

Answer: lion, ladybug, leaf, lobster, leopard

Where Do You Live?—/l/
Just For Kids: Articulation Stories

/l/ Picture Search   Name _____

Find at least five things that have an /l/ sound in the middle of the word. Circle them.

Family: Please practice the /l/ sound in:

☐ words—Say each /l/ picture _____ times.

☐ sentences—Make up _____ sentences about each /l/ picture.

☐ conversation—Talk about the picture. What other zoo animals have an /l/ sound?

Answer: tulips, elephant, alligator, caterpillar, balloon, smiling

/l/ Picture Search   Name _____

Find at least five things that have an /l/ sound at the end of the word. Circle them.

Family: Please practice the /l/ sound in:

☐ words—Say each /l/ picture _____ times.

☐ sentences—Make up _____ sentences about each /l/ picture.

☐ conversation—Talk about the picture. Have you ever been to a water show?

Answer: whale, tail, ball, squirrel, owl

Where Do You Live?—/l/
Just For Kids: Articulation Stories

/l/ Writing Activity   Name _____

In the story, "Where Do You Live?", the animals live in places with an /l/ sound.

Think of places that have an /l/ sound. Here are some ideas to get you started: lake, bowling alley, pool, library.

☐ Draw a picture of one of these places.

☐ Write about it.

_____
_____
_____
_____
_____

/l/ Barrier Game

Name _____

Use this page with page 171.

/l/ Barrier Game, continued

Cut out the animals and put them in their homes on page 170.

Where Do You Live?—/l/
Just For Kids: Articulation Stories

Sample Tracking Form—Productions

Name: **Molly Smith** Date: **October 8** Target Phoneme: **/s/**

Circle the appropriate position and level. Use the key to record accuracy of productions and any cueing and models provided.

+ correct	IM immediate model
– incorrect	DM delayed model
° tactile cueing	NM no model
✓ visual cueing	

Position	Level		Production
(initial), medial, final, blends	(word), phrase, sentence, conversation	IM	+ + + + + + + + + + 10/10
		DM	+ – + + – + – + + + 7/10
		NM	not attempted
initial, (medial), final, blends	(word), phrase, sentence, conversation	IM	+✓ – +✓ +✓ +✓ – +✓ +✓ +✓ – 7/10—needs visual cueing
		DM	not attempted
		NM	not attempted
initial, medial, (final), blends	(word), phrase, sentence, conversation	IM	+✓ +✓ +✓ – +✓ +✓ +✓ – +✓ +✓ 8/10—needs visual cueing
		DM	not attempted
		NM	not attempted
initial, medial, final, (blends)	(word), phrase, sentence, conversation	IM	+°✓ +°✓ –✓ +°✓ +°✓ +°✓ –✓ +°✓ +°✓ +°✓ 8/10—needs visual and tactile cueing
		DM	not attempted
		NM	not attempted

Just For Kids: Articulation Stories

Tracking Form—Productions

Name _____ Date _____ Target Phoneme _____

Circle the appropriate position and level. Use the key to record accuracy of productions and any cueing and models provided.

+ correct	IM immediate model
− incorrect	DM delayed model
° tactile cueing	NM no model
✓ visual cueing	

Position	Level		Production
initial medial final blends	word phrase sentence conversation	IM DM NM	
initial medial final blends	word phrase sentence conversation	IM DM NM	
initial medial final blends	word phrase sentence conversation	IM DM NM	
initial medial final blends	word phrase sentence conversation	IM DM NM	

Sample Tracking Form—Percentages

Name: Molly Smith   Target Phoneme: /s/

Plot correct percentages of production by word position. (Dashed lines indicate change of model and/or cueing provided.)

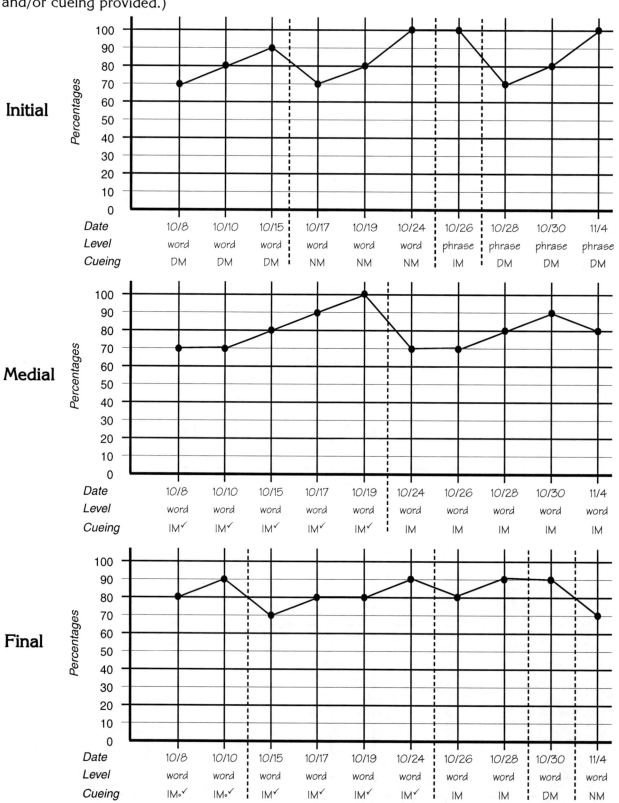

Tracking Form—Percentages

Name _____ Target Phoneme _____

Plot correct percentages of production by word position.

Initial

Percentages: 0, 10, 20, 30, 40, 50, 60, 70, 80, 90, 100

Date
Level
Cueing

Medial

Percentages: 0, 10, 20, 30, 40, 50, 60, 70, 80, 90, 100

Date
Level
Cueing

Final

Percentages: 0, 10, 20, 30, 40, 50, 60, 70, 80, 90, 100

Date
Level
Cueing

Just For Kids: Articulation Stories